My Two Sense

Peter Cherry

Written by Peter Cherry
Audio performed and produced by Peter Cherry
Illustration by Peter Cherry
Edited by Peter Cherry; Edited by Kalisha D. Lemmitt-Cherry.
Copy Editor Peter Cherry
2023 and 2024 Angelic Reign, Inc. Publication
Copyright and Trademarked original print 2003 and 2017;
revised 2023 digital print 2012 and 2017; revised 2023; 2024
and audio 2017 by Peter Cherry and Angelic Reign, Inc.

ISBN: 979-8-9902578-5-6

Table of Contents

Dedications

Dear Lord, Thank you.
To you the glory.
Amen.
To my parents- For all that you have done
for me. Thank you.
To my sisters and brothers.
Thank you.
To the rest of my family and friends.
Thank you.
In memory of loved ones that have passed
on. Thank you.

A Thought

As a child, all you know is your parents.

As a child, you learn to explore and gain friendships;
mostly with others your same age or background.

Your level of understanding things begins to grow.

You will be introduced to education; politics; religion;
and pop culture.

As a teenager, you start searching for something,
but don't have the slightest idea of what it is.

It's normally labeled rebellion; weird; or just trying to fit in.

Actually, you're trying to know yourself.

As a young adult, your world expands on the outside.

Question the future.

Is it what you want, or what you think you might want?

Life becomes a series of stages created by judgments
and just guessing.

This, of course, is just the way of our society.

If you want to change, you must do three things:

1.Look within yourself.

2.Be honest with yourself.

3.Never stop loving yourself.

We all possess the power of change.

A lot of us forget the power exists.

Life

Life is filled with countless paths and endless directions.

Any way we turn leads us into many different lives.

Each one different from the last, with the possibility of having a minor similarity or two.

No matter how economically advanced, or socially deprived.

Life is a gift that should never be taken for granted.

-Cherish it-

In life, things don't suppose to come easy;

to decline the challenge will lead you

into an empty void of uncertainty.

Live, Love, Learn, and **Grow.**

Family

Many branches stimulating from a single tree.
The hopes and dreams of relatives
seen and unseen.
Architects, constantly building upon
monuments of love.
Teachers of knowledge and life.
Comfort from the pain and the strife.
Everything and still so much more.

Guidance and Insight

My Pops told me,
"Do as I say.
Don't do as I did.
Just enjoy being a kid."
"That's my lil' dude!"
"I will be real with you."
"When you get older,
you can take my words and
use them for what it's worth."
"It will be on you to choose, my son."
Training has begun.
Teaching me rules, calling it guidance.
The inspiration for my reign is my pops,
the "original" royal king highness.
I must confess,I get the best from my mom.
She told me,
"Realize and recognize your spirit and worth."
"You can't take care of no one unless
you know how to take care of yourself first!"

Discipline

wer: The ability to bend things in your favor: control.

ed properly, can build; unify;

aling the masses within a split of a second.

ed improperly, can manipulate and cripple a clouded society;

iving a person to be corrupt; unsure of one's self-worth;

iming the true duty of power;

ning the most magnificent to the most shame.

uth: The correct answer to any question or deed;

ither good nor bad; just is.

ed wisely, can open mental eyes to an unknown: validate.

ed improperly, can be infected with false and twisted

srepresentation for selfish convictions.

spect: The ability to be looked upon with esteem

one's self or group.

ed properly, can cultivate minds; enrich the soul;

acing one on an equal chord.

ed improperly, can reduce a person in regards;

humanize; being placed in a lower level; a mistreated vessel.

sponsibility: accountability for deeds done or undone.

ed properly, helps with moral growth.

ed improperly, can cripple any structure and weaken perspectives.

Love: A bond that gathers and captures
moments or lifetimes.
Used properly, can build spiritual growth; patience;
character;and understanding.
Used improperly, can overly stress;
confuse; weaken forethought.

My First Friend

My first friend was introduced into my life as a stranger.

Uninterested in my rantings and ravings,

but intrigued by my thoughts.

My first friend wasn't interested in the things I had.

The only interest was what's truly in my heart.

My first friend never pacified my feelings,

just made them stronger.

We don't see eye to eye, sometimes.

I'm blessed to have someone like you in my life.

Dedicated to…

Ambition

I can feel it in my hands.
Constantly, reading and remembering
actual papers, literally for literarily learning.
The past; the present, the future is like my high,
slightly hazy.
Placing them into a diploma,
when the world's stress attempts to shake me.
It would be a mistake for me to let anxiety break me.
As my ambition lights way,
I take a deep breath, because to day is my day!

Preparing Myself

Tell me my destiny, or can it be I make my own way?
Back in the day, my grandpa told me
it was important to learn the lessons in life.
"I'm trying!"
It's scary knowing the world can be
cold and rusty as a knife.
"Really!"
What's life without a taste of strife?
Perhaps my legacy is my journey.
The money, a tool to be used for thrills and bills.
Lord, it's in your will to give me something real to feel.
Please keep me in your arms, protecting me from harm.
Amen.

On Your Shoulder

"Who the hell are you?"

"From hell, can't you tell?!

Notorious for evil giggling

and keeping innocent people in jail.

The one who inspired Poe's

anxiety to write the Tell-Tale.

No soul, just an empty shell.

Just turn your back and power shall dwell."

"Alright."

"You that easy?"

"You really need some insight."

"Who are you?"

"I'm the light.

I'm the inspiration; the guardian.

Protecting the kids and the adults at night;

keeping your soul away from evil.

I'm prepared to fight.

I love you, but you not so bright."

"That's not nice!"

"Forget what you just heard.

Don't listen to that nerd.

I got what you want: lust, power, and greed."

"Really, that sounds good to me!"

"To make it official just bleed on the deed!"

"Don't take that chance better ask what it costs
or you will find yourself lost!"

"Who made you the boss?!"

"You're not the leader either.
The final decision ends with the reader."

Where I've Been

I never been around the world.

I've dipped through a few corners.

Looking at how we put a lot stress upon us.

I'm just a single spirit among a vast sea of souls.

As an animal called man,

aren't we suppose to live by a code?

Yet, we let our own people die in the cold.

Still, within the end I have faith in our cause.

We may not know what it is.

That's why we're stuck in a pause.

Ask yourself.

"Is he writing what is real?"

If you can feel, then yeah, it's real!

My understanding of life may have started on time;

impatience made it seem the idea showed up late.

The stress of growing up felt like

a two-hundred- pound weight. Wait!

I know I can lift it.

Blessed with good sense; a recognized heart; and gifted.

So be cool, stay up,

and maybe one day we will get it and wake up.

For now, this is how it is.

Good luck.

Eye Opener

Everybody's got secrets to keep.

Rather you did dirt or doing dirt,

better be mindful some of your skeletons have feet.

Be mindful of the company you keep.

If you're mentally sleep, that gives the thief time to creep.

Take a look at the people on your block.

Some of y'all only cool because you are the only one who

shared what you got.

Life can be hard as a boulder.

While the world can make situations seem a lot colder.

Who really wants to spend the rest of their days

looking over their shoulder?

Stress

Anxiety fills concentrated drama through reality viewed sites.

Jealousy is the blame for misplace shame; seeking fame;

and taking a bow under the malice lights.

Mine are simple illustrations, intended for the world to view.

Praising and giving it to God as a sacrifice,

sometimes our continuous convictions dwell

the demons we are intended to fight.

Crippled with fright of the unknown within our sights,

we lash out at others out of spite; constantly avoiding

the mirror containing the image we don't like.

God, bless the ones who feel they face their troubles alone.

Lord, protect all of our children, especially the ones away from home.

Lord, have mercy towards those who hurt others, especially themselves.

Lord God, please walk with me on my path of knowing thyself.

Can't Cope

Lord, please! There's a blessing in need?!
I'm stuck within this street life,
I feel so closed in I can't even breathe.
My baby needs diapers.
My family and friends are gone.
All I need is a couple of answers.
I don't mean to do wrong,
Can't you see!
I'm down on my knees, praying for release.
I saw my boy die turning into a beast of greed.
There is no honor among thieves.
I got to hustle to pay bills, or what I call fleas.
Guide me please!
I feel my end; this only started because I was broken.
Is there a ghetto in heaven for a man that can't cope?!

Lady in Black

Lady in black,

are you still wearing that dress?!

He has been gone for so long and you're still upset.

The taste of bitter rain reigned after he left.

Damning yourself in constant pain carries a strain

worse than any death.

Bitterness!

Is it at times you feel so cold?

Swinging on reality, but have no hold?

People still love you.

Let your heart and mind guide you!

I'm not able to predict the future.

Time may make it easier, with positive support.

"For every ending there is a beginning."

Just Kids

As an adult, going through life is all I know.

I express love for my parents, they allowed me to grow.

The aim is about the kids!

Let me explain.

As adults, we have to be mindful of what we put in their brains.

Kids ain't kids no more!

The meaning of childhood has changed.

Who's the blame?

Quit pointing fingers and naming names!

Every day we lose a child by wrapping them up in our mess;

they wear the drama like chains.

It's too heavy!

So inside themselves they can't help but to sink to the bottom.

Save them fast!

Before something bad could happen.

Worse, your baby could be dead in the dirt!

Too much hurt?

How about stealing out of momma's purse? Or, hear them curse,

"I don't give a damn about my daddy!"

Who is he?"

"I run this here! Oh, yeah, I need some money."
When I raise mine,
I'm going to love them and tell them how it is.
I will do right by them and allow them to grow.
Why?
They are just kids.

Ain't Safe

It ain't safe no more!

From a history standpoint, when was it even safe before?

In libraries and stores are books about women and men

that were discredited, tortured or killed for their beliefs.

A noted issue which still remains the same.

"Where is peace?"

If someone of my same skin commits a

wrong act in the streets,

I'm automatically judged based off "that" profile I meet.

When was it ever truly safe to practice a religious faith

without a big debate?

Warring and getting on each other's case,

like bragging rights on which is,

"The one true faith."

I'll wait until judgment day;

God will tell me.

Is it all a schism on the fear of what people

don't know?

With so much organized confusion and control,

I'd rather stay to myself and pray for my own Soul.

More Than You

Stop your ill! Rewind, mind frame sick.

Pre-judging!

I feel inclined to introduce a fear of what you don't know.

Get a grip and hold on.

Expand your mind and grow on.

It's more than your world and so forth and so on.

Here's an idea.

Imagine yourself facing a jury in court.

You are about to go to jail because everyone in the jury
is a vegetarian,

and they know you eat pork.Of course, not everyone is out
to understand or get it.

I'm only speaking real, there are a lot of people that live it!

Hate's Speech

"My name is Hate;
 I don't like you."
"I've been here since your ancestors,
first fought over bananas. The bastard children…"
"I am the seed of ignorance and fear;
I've made countries at odds over land.
The world is my personal sandlot."
"I made the crucifixion possible so a few
priests and politicians could feel like they kept their so called,
"power."
Avoiding change at their twisted expense,
I love their insecurities."
"My favorite pastime is listening to bitter people talk with disdain;
aving their hurt replay in their heads, looped like a video,
and it's breaking their spirits, so there is no reason left."
"Making them hate who don't look like them or act like them.
Like an outbreak that spreads every five seconds.
You humans are weak, how can you be loved above others?!"
"I hate you!"
 "I can fill you up with vile to make you hate yourself.
Never were you in control, my little meat puppet.
Prideful primitives, you're neither the beginning nor ending.
Just a rusty tool that I've used for centuries to be divided,
letting me reign over you."

"Stupid;

Clouded;

Addictive;

Emotional;

Unstable

Humanity."

I Am

Call me Mr. Nice; my suggestion,

think twice once in your life.

If you ever believe that you could punk or play me.

Step up and try it!

I'll point you this way.

Why don't you be a good kid; go away and play.

I'm one of the dirtiest of dirt dogs!

I can do this all day.

Anyway…

I came to say, "I love Mom & Pops!"

They taught me the game when they exclaimed,

"You will be perceived as ghetto, so use your brain!"

"Some things look different, but it still means the same!"

"Forget all the hype and infamous fame."

"I send you out in this world; my son, do your thang."

My parents put me on the path and placed the tools in my hand.

So here I stand.

Untitled

You sunk so low?
Lower than a dollar laying flat on the floor?
Under and drowning, wishing your problems could go?
Truly though!
Do I suppose to understand this life you living?
Who told you it was cool to be lying and stealing?
Aren't motivated on nothing, saying you're
wheeling and dealing.
When was it cool to be beating on women?
Claiming you a pimp, you are straight tripping!
Got your hand out, never willing to help yourself.
Dressed down all the way down,
still with nothing to show for yourself.
Perhaps you don't know what it's like to give it your all
until you got nothing left!
Even with your last breath, you strive to take another step.
So, how dare you have the audacity to get mad at me!
Then disguise it with fake love; to me, it's like a Blasphemy!
Stories full of contradictions, sounding like lies to me!
I'm only giving you what you asked to see.
The Truth.

Regardless

When the war comes, damn right,
I'm coming battle ready!
This isn't anytime to pack light! I travel heavy!
I try to be cool, then dumb asses try to test me!
I lost control, and only the Lord can save me!
I was fine until a fool made the mistake to cross me.
Family?!
Aw, damn this lesson is costly!
Obviously!
Rage and hurt are what I'm serving, that's automatic.
I can't believe you came this way to start some static?!
War, you going to have it!
You know how we were raised, and now heartless
is the habit!
My weapon of choice?
Oh, no! You will never grasp it!
You think that you can truly keep me down?
Too bad; so sad.
Asking for trouble; round for round.
Trying to be civilized; before the Lord I bow down.
I do more than just growl when I smile, I'm a hound!
Regardless I'm defending mine!

Lost It

Instead of yelling, "Damn the world!"
I'm screaming, "Damn your life!" There was never a rope.
I warned you before; I quit being nice.
The next step is me sticking this knife in your windpipe!
My doctor's telling me, "Quit getting so hype."
"Don't throw away your potential going to jail over a fight.
I suggest anger management."
Whatever!
I'll be alright.
Like the electric company,
I'm about to turn off some lights!
Demons driving me to the edge; my ambition is to fight!
Can't control myself; I'm losing the light!
Will you pray for me now;
or wait until I enter the night?
This ain't right!
I'm losing sight.

Talking Wild

I can get you hyped if I said,

"Raise them high, or throw it up!"

I can also get you hyped if I said,

"I don't give a ...!"

If you understand,

welcome to the world in God we trust.

If you don't understand,

like stepping in the mud; you stuck.

You got money long.

All you do is pass the buck.

"Hold up!"

Simply, say,

"Human is our race!"

Is our nature only to destroy and create?

It's a necessary evil to harbor hate?

Jealousy is just our animalistic,

urge to help us survive and take!

"Waste…"

Crazy

Some brains on Kane, my mind ain't Able.
I'm just idle with nothing to do except mess with you.
Trapped in a moment of maniac melancholy,
something's wrong with the cable.
Labeled mental; strange; and unstable.
Crazy probably; maybe I need some medicine.
I got a story about a spot that just got hot
with me in the spotlight,
with a bunch of people gathered in the lot
where the cars are parked.
Just before the brightest of dispatch,
a streetlight provided a sign to shine on me
when I wished I was one with the dark.
Not being so smart, the rest of the area
was pretty much all dark.
All because this dude
collapsed coming out the club clutching his heart.
Towards him, I darted.
Expired eyes replied his soul had left.
I scavenged,
repossessing the necklace he had draped around
his neck. Rather unwise; unlucky; disrespectful;
or unblessed.

Now a crowd has formed around us because
the club just closed down. Now more spectators around…
I know I'm under arrest.
Instantly, caught up in some mess!
Lord, forgive my plea;
Please, one small request to have
 a window of opportunity left....
I have to kiss the lips of death; blowing breaths,
performing CPR on his chest.
Nervous as shit, at best.
I'm terrified;all I could do was look into his eyes,
telling me the story of his demise…
"Surprise!"
"It's the Mack King of keeping heavy stacks,
and I'm back to make it rain!
Here's my five dollas;
let me inside the club bitch- it's on again!"
"Doing my thang!"
"Aye;
where that chick at that let me and One-Eye run that train?
A sad shame!
She was awarded thirty dollars,
a trophy, and got her picture framed…"
"I- won't- ever change!"
"Over access is the fuel in my tank! "
"Hey girl, you cute, but your breath stank!"
"I'm just being a creep; why don't you buy me a drink?"
"Let me ask you something and you tell me what you think?
My crack   head brother...Aye, are you listening?

I said my crackhead brother stole my needles.

For a week I haven't taken my insulin, I'm weak.

I've been taking pills just to boost my adrenalin."

"Wow! Feeling lightheaded and hot!
I'm gonna get some air, then come back
and order six shots!"

Walking from the table to the door, "It's hot!"
"Hard to catch… a… breath."

He took five steps and collapsed, clutching his chest.

"Oh God, not like this!"
"Not by myself!"
"Here comes someone."
"Aw hell naw! He taking my chain?!"
"Damn messed up shame!"
Even worse, if I was him,
I would have done the same messed up thang."

"Oh, hell!" "Well, I gave somebody a story to tell…"

The Sermon

Listen, my people listen!"
I had an interesting conversation with a brother
hat got out of jail and turned his life around."
He got an education; started a successful business;
nd moved his family out of poverty; and everyone is doing good."
Then he proceeded to tell me he went down
ɔ the old neighborhood, and it looked like a deserted ghost town.
Now, don't get me wrong; the brother is a good man,
ut I got pissed!!!"
How in the hell you gone talk about the condition
when you yourself had a part in messing it up!"
He looked at me like, 'Damn, Preacher!'"
Instead of tea or 'coool-aid', call me straight with no chaser!"
You took without regard of the neighborhood
ou was in for whatever your reason!"
You matured and moved on without replenishing
what you took, and you dare wonder why it looks this way?!"
That's like your fifteen-year-old spilling cereal on the floor,
nd wonder when you gonna clean it up!"
What the Hell!!"

"Yes, I did say, 'What the Hell!'"

"The Lord was with me because,
I could have chosen other letters."

"Then the look he gave me was like
he was about to judge me turned into,
'Damn! My bad!'"

"I am not here to scold you or judge you; that is
not my job."

"Just please realize your impact shapes this world
even if this world didn't impact and shape
you as you would have liked."

"Change just don't come in the morning;
it comes with a thought and a commitment."

"Do you hear what I'm saying?!"

The Game

True playas of the game use strategies and plans.
The whole meaning of it is to gain the upper hand.
You may claim to be one of the best in the game.
Somebody can play it a little bit better all the same.
You can be a casualty if you let a game become all you do.
In this world, you're not the only one confused.
People only know what you give them access to know.
So just sit back and let reality grow.
If you're suffering from this type of paranoia,
that's a damn SHAME!

Pimp'n Honey

It's kinda funny.
Before we started Pimp'n Honey.
She was a down and out freak.
Honey loved the money.
When I came around, I was silly.
We started to act chummy.
Gaming from the start,
she thought I was a dummy.
Gaming from the start, "I'm good.
Honey your scent is yummy."
Why play a game?
We know we can.
It ain't my fault if she mistakes me for the other.
Bad man?
Understand, Honey had a plan.
Loose-a-man-gain-a-man just because she can.
Perhaps the last man took her heart, dropped it,
and dashed.
Me, all I want is some… She's fast on the rebound.
Sex her body; and clown.

Time kept ticking;
after a while look what I have found.
I actually got to know her.
Better keep my feelings down.
We built each other up; happy to have you.
Always a smile and never a frown.
Perhaps in our minds,
both of us were wondering,
"How long will the other one be around?"

Gossip

I can keep a secret! Please tell me what do you fear?"
"Wait right here."
"Aye! Everybody, I have some gossip!"
"Open your ears."
I know how to take a person and reduce them to tears."
First,
"Aye, you!
Please, come here."
You bring them out in front of their peers.
"Hi!"
"Don't be afraid, you're in front of friends here."
"Aye!"
"Y'all!"
"Cheer or clap, join in or something!"
"Anyway."
"I heard you caught your wife at home
with another man, fixing her plumbing."

"I heard you still don't know who the daddy is.
Only two days remain, then the baby is coming."
"Ain't that something!?"
"I also heard you got passed around.
Now you're labeled a sick trick."
This is for those that love to talk like this.
"Who the hell are you!?"
Ya'll really need to quit.
How are you talking about somebody,
when you need to check your shit?
"Don't have a fit!"
I just placed you in a zone.
Who wants to be first to throw some stones?
"Oh! I forgot!"
Misery loves company,
of course you wouldn't want to be alone.

Is It Love?

If I say,
"Babe, you and I fit tighter than a hand'n glove."
Then I bruise and shed blood with them same gloves.
Is it Love?
If I rob you of your self-esteem,
constantly reassuring that you are beneath me.
When you try to leave,
I'm constantly praising you as my queen.
Is it Love?
If I try to separate you from the ones
that care about you the most.
Is it Love?
Knowing that I don't want you,
but I don't want anyone else to have you.
I decide to play and keep you.
Is it Love?

Fool

She gave me the keys to the houses;
access to the cars;
money in my pocket;
clothes from the stores.
Always looking for what's hot;
running in and out of spots.
Addicted to too much shit; trying to get
before it's got gladly.
I was broke as a joke.
Nobody on her side liked me.
Forget getting a job; I just got keep giving her my
long stroking miraculously,
I'm acting with no regard.
I should stop;
I can't because it's too damn hard.
Forget cutting the front and backyards,
unless we talking about her anatomy…
in a moment she's gonna be more than mad at me…

Dear Love,
A lesson like astronomy,
I learned that we are worlds apart.
Our history, plus my countless recesses, isn't reuniting us togeth
I failed our chemistry to love our art.
From the start, we shaped conversations;
spoke feelings from the heart.
I remember you said,"Men will be men.
Just respect me enough not to leave me in the dark."
I did what I did alone; with selfish pride;feeding the birds in the
I misused you; lied about the other women I messed with.
Now regretful, a shadow of your memory is what I'm left with.
All these issues I bear are hard… you deserve the truth.
Oh Poochie, at times, when you were kissing me
you tasting your cousin's coo... I know it shouldn't have taken pl
when I finished, I left wiping my face.
I was ashamed of myself; so is your cousin Beth.
You told her about the sex and she wanted to find out for herself
I will never find another; just know I wouldn't do it over.
I would be a lie if I said you weren't on my mind.
Every time I close my eyes, seeing your pretty face.
I start to grin, then begin to cringe when
I think about the mistakes that made the heartache
for which you went away.
How I feel, still...
I walk in the rain, replaying scenes in my head
that placed tears slowly flowing down your face.
Still in the end, I want my love; my friend for me.
You made my world a beautiful place.
I'm leaving you; be if you only knew the grief
in my heart that dwells such a lonely place.

Is it Respect?

If she treats you less than, demeaning you.
Then in the same breath says, "I love you,"
just to receive something while she goes out
giving it to somebody else.
Is it Respect?
If she expects you to understand,
after she got caught up or pregnant;
quietly avoiding or lying about the other man.
Is it Respect?
Her mind thinking that you are going to leave her,
so she tries to hold something over your head.
Making you stay just to keep problems down.
Is it Respect?
You think you're receiving,
when she doesn't know how to respect herself.
Just asking…

Storm Confusion

For twelve days now,
especially on the first day, remember it rained?
I felt strange for a while knowing that
something had changed.
Replaying scenes in my brain.
Thinking, then avoiding.
No, I need to be realistic;
I got to put it all together.
What we have is real.
We can move away from this "thing."
I believe we could last forever!
However,…
I wish we could have reigned together.
I guess we didn't have what it took to
brace for the stormy weather. Whatever.
I guess that's how the game goes.
Naw.
I guess the ending changed from the beginning.
"Friends," or so I thought.
We started off wrong, who cares!
I felt the love showed.
Both of us were committed to being,
"Scared of commitment type" hoes.
Young minded...

Service Announcement from Gentlemen

The worst misconception some women have is thinking they always
got the game and gone with it.
Rethink yourself.
You are now being introduced to a gentleman/real man
and not our stand-ins 'elementary-minded pretenders' aka "busters.
Ladies, as lovely; moist; and delicious as it is,
the power of pussy is overrated.
When your being manipulative just to play a game.
False sense of security for some.
To be honest, saying men want sex is like stating water is wet.
Every man, whether well-mannered; uncouth; religious; atheist; poor
or rich,wants to have sex with the female they are trying to get next to.
What you should look for is how it's presented
and not the fact we may want it.
Ladies, men aren't checking for
what's in-between; actually,
what's up top.
"Where's your head at?"
To know that dictates how we deal with you; separating
the ladies from the "not ready," aka "bitches."
Note: you can have three or more kids; on Section 8; with somebody
living in the basement, and still be a lady.
Just like you can own your company; no kids;
independence is your nickname, and still be trifling.
It's not your situation but your attitude.
When a lady/real woman are comfortable and naturally vibing with us
she will have more of an enjoyable moment getting to know the man.
Regardless, if it leads to a long-term relationship
or just going out from time to time.
How she is being treated; most important is she having fun, stands out.

The issue of money is no issue when going out because whatever you choose to do is just scenery; everything else is the lady and gent.

Not ready ladies/stand-ins' normally seem emotionally lost

and can't grasp the idea of an "overly" nice man.

Caution: you're fucking up already!

A man doesn't have to curse you out or worse to prove something.

If you decide to practice a user mentality in order to play the game of, "Let me see how far he is going let me take it,"

this may result in you getting your feelings hurt by reality.

You are not entitled to anything!

He just likes you, that's all.

If dealing with you is like a chore, or a bunch of bank machine dates, a money dog will buy you; use you; and be gone.

Gangstas will use you; fuck over you; and be gone.

Pimps automatically say you're out of pocket.

Then there's the nice guy.

He will be cool around you; might hang around you for a minute;

and won't stay around long because he will feel like

you are trying to use him.

If you exhibit this type of behavior, be careful.

Rethink, or you will find yourself by yourself.

Stop being a stand- in!

Hopefully, this will help you identify us a little better;

and if we show interest, and display persistence, we are not a stalker.

Just to say you are worth pursuing is a good thing.

By men being nervous and trying a little hard, you can feel that vibe.

He still wants to impress you and does not want to mess up a good thin

You have his undivided attention; tell him to chill and breath.

When you see our vulnerable or

sensitive side, our guards are down with you.

That means you are in… quit looking for other shit!

Since we don't advertise our feels in magazines, we do
hold group discussions online.
You won't really know unless a gentleman lets you know,
or you have been around one long enough to know.
At least now you can say you have
barely scratched the surface.

Ain't Ready

I refused to be used, confused, abused,
or just stuck being a crutch.
Disappointed and crushed,
Who gonna hold me down if I go mentally nuts?
Bullshit can wait in the rain and still miss the bus.
My eyes are closed and opened; in God I trust.
Recently, I got my heart broken;
I got a barrier up like a fence.
Why did I give her my heart?
Damn, I haven't been right since!
What's love anyway?
Can anybody explain it!?
Is it capturing moments in time,
so we can picture and frame it?
Everybody got issues; it's only a few
that want to try to change it.
Love's a gamble.
I'd rather gather my chips.
Change the game?
More affordable to get brain.
Besides, this is not poker;
cutting with spades or holding all the jokers.
Making all the books, counting all the overs
Under bid that's a lie!

I ran out of hearts; Baby, rise and fly.

Tired and retired from love; the game's over.

I'm cool. Other people are cutthroat,

with moves a hundred times colder.

All the women want to fight him,

and all the dudes want to choke her.

Relationships like these always invite the law over.

Look at the time.

Thanks for inviting me over.

No good.

Aren't you the one that made drama our final closure?

Screw you, be safe, and watch out for posers.

What do you do, when love tests to be false?

Poor Love, you must be lost.

Must have been sleep on the bus,

because this is not your stop!

Besides,

I'm too busy to deal with you love right now.

Invested and doing me is

the best thing going right about now.

Can't fall in it now!

Love at least for a while;

I'm still missing her smile.

Eye Opener 'Bluntly Stated'

How many men yelled out,
"Dirty bitch!"
How many women said,
"Weak ass men ain't shit!"
How many people are in drug court
for dirty piss?
 "Damn!"
This is for those who realize this stuff.
What are you gonna do?
Be silent and stay on the hush?
Holler out, "The hell with this!"
Makes you want and get your ass on a bus?
Better yet, get drunk and go back,
shaking your head; still pondering,
"What the fuck?!"
For the ones that choose to stay,
I would like to wish you luck.

Advice

To stay in love in certain situations
is usually easier said than done.
Some might agree dealing with the pain
is like a shot from emotions gun.
I've heard of a lot of stories where someone felt
things would get "better" having a little girl or boy.
That's dumb!
Be wise and open your eyes;
never use a child as a disguise.
You may even say the words,
Love's in your mind they feel like lies.
I'm crazy! Still, your reasoning sounds strange to me.
Perhaps the true answer resides in you.
After all of the advice,
What do you want to do and need to do are different?
-Choices-

Tears

Walking in the park crying,
my tears are hidden within the mist of the rain.
Why this day!
All I know is her.
The beginning of love was her.
Lord, why did you take her away from me!?
"Shhh, my darling Grandbaby."
"I thanked the Lord for giving me each moment with you."
"Your love lifted me up each moment of every day."
'You were always here, now I'm afraid;
I feel lost without you.'
"Through life you have to learn to face your
fears and endure some pain.
Mine was not being able to wipe away your tears."
"Baby, just hold on to faith; in your heart,
I will always stay."
"I ask the Lord to give you a hug and kiss
for me every time I pray."
"I love you always by night and by day."

Pain

I wish I could just fly away!

I was deceived; taken advantage of;

broken; and betrayed.

Should I fly away?

Hell, naw!

I'm going to stay.

I was underestimated anyway!

Face to face.

Don't take kindness for a weakness,

using behind my back sneakiness.

Watch me reach to this higher level in me never seen before.

Realize and recognize.

You don't know me anymore, or rather,

did you think you actually knew me from before?!

I never thought to shed any tears, ya know?

My pain nourishes my spirit to grow.

The Reign

My reign consists of travels; challenges;
inspirations; and pain.
My foundation of love; joy; and ambition intensifies
my inner dimensions for change.
Who am I?
The lighting you see when it is about to rain.
The first thing you felt when your skeletons came.
Genesis 4, in my opinion, is the introduction to the
"game."
My heart is like the serenity prayer.
If you ever wonder do I care?
Look at my middle finger I got posted in the air.
"It's not good to swear!"
Neither is beating yourself with a chain.
My actions are lame only if your aim is the same.
The strategy of life can be like a chess game.
"So, what are your moves?"
For you, it will be more of the same.
Sit back and relax; you'll put your mind in a strain.
Just being me.
That's why I call it, 'The Reign.'

Too Much of Many

Too much skepticism;
I need not quit.
Too many haters;
I got to shake them now,
and shake them later.
Too much work is making my head hurt.
Too many times, I quoted this!

Faith

From the start,

the Lord has blessed me with an open mind, and a loving heart.

After a kiss on my forehead,

God said that my lessons in life will come in parts.

"REMEMBER, I MADE YOU UNIQUE."

"THAT'S HOW I SET MY CHILDREN APART."

"Dear Lord, what if I don't understand my lessons and fall by the wayside? What if,

I'm not strong enough to succeed?"

"MY CHILD, PUT DOWN YOUR BURDENS OF STONE.

I WILL NEVER LEAVE YOU ALONE."

"I'M YOUR ROCK;

YOUR STRENGHTH;

YOUR GUIDING LIGHT TO FIND YOUR WAY HOME."

"Lord, I know I'm not perfect, yet in still you love me so!"

"Where others have broken me, you have always made me whole."

Salvation

One learns from life's lessons;
some may live and teaches the true values of the lessons.
Keeping accountability for their actions;
standing firm when need be.
Stay rich in spirit,
gain respect and love from others by the power of one's heart.
Wise to know nothing will be gained; to inherit everything,
just to lose yourself.
Imperfect; holding the potential for greatness.
Are blessed and humbled to know they are made in
the image of the creator...
Dear Lord,
I'm feeling stressed and frustrated with life's lessons and tests.
In this hysteria, whom did you favor best?
After the rain, the pain will go.
Serenity's gift is learning to let it go.

Heart of Hearts

With a Heart of Hearts,
We never want to see things fall apart.
With a Heart of Hearts,
we supposed to stay true to ourselves;
as we find our parts before the hell begins to start.
Lies; deception; and no self-worth!
My Heart of Hearts,
if this is what you're offering me,
I'll return it back; for real, you can have it.
Respect doesn't mean you got to start some static!
With a Heart of Hearts,
standing on your own is a habit!
With a Heart of Hearts,
we pray to the Lord, at any time, or place.
All we got is our faith!
Never let the demons pull us away from grace!

Appreciate

I appreciate myself!
As long as I have the Lord,
I don't need no one else!
I appreciate my mind.
I appreciate my eyes.
I appreciate my face.
My height; my hair; my weight.
I appreciate my faith in myself.
No matter how the haters hate.
I'm safe in the grace.
Can't think of a better place.
That's why…
I appreciate myself!
As long as I have the Lord,
I don't need no one else!
I appreciate my voice.
I appreciate my tone.
I appreciate my thoughts.
When I talk literally,
expressing my stance.

As I walk holding my bearings,

more funerals than graduations or weddings.

Hypnotized by false words, used by doubters,

Who I allowed to use my fears as a weapon.

I get on my knees,

"O' Lord thank you!

You hold the power!"

I appreciate myself!

As long as I have the Lord,

I don't need no one else!

I appreciate my style.

I appreciate my flow.

I appreciate having an enlightened soul.

With my shield and sword says,

I appreciate that I'm blessed.

I appreciate myself!

As long as I have the Lord,

I don't need no one else!

Mmm

This is the world.

Where, mankind can marvel in the genius of science; religion; and political structure.

Still blinded by money; lust; power; and convenience.

A place where medical achievements occur every day.

Never seeing ourselves as equals.

Since I told you about the kind of world we live in, get over it and handle your business!

Presidential

My fellow Americans,
I am a businessman; and so are
the government officials you support for elections.
Our job is to represent the interest of the people
who live here, and trade with our neighbors across the globe.
Like with any businessman,
I have been interested in numbers
and the endeavors of my associates.
As a man, I have been selfish, and, at times, bullheaded.
I lost track of the things that are truly important: "life."
Even though everyone has different viewpoints on what's,
"living" to them, we are all family;
 "dysfunctional," yet still a family.
Our ancestors created and carried racism and placism
through decades like a banner for pain.
Where is the pride, knowing that the people fight for work and
frustrated; angry; overly used; and under appreciated?
Where's the pride in screaming, "Educate,"
while systematically breaking down the quality and foundatio
just for the sake of politics; prestige; or money?
Where is the pride?

Pointing the finger at someone,
without placing it first upon you???
We are all aware this is a world truly divided
by the haves and the have nots.
I have money; you have not.
You have faith; I have not.
I have accessibility; you have not.
You have morals; I have not.
I have to think about my family; and think of yours not.
Crazy is the prophet who speaks of destruction.
I also say, insane is the society that embraces
the systematic divides between us all.
In all lands,we state things in the name of the Lord.
It is blasphemy to incorporate the Lord's name with killing;
lying; worshiping false idols; wars; political bureaucracy;
and deception for material wants.
God intended greater things for us all, not the few.
I'm not going to state we need chaos to build leaders,
oreveryone hold hands.
I will say we need to rethink everything;
our society; families; and most important, ourselves.
So talented; methodical.
Strong; yet so misguided.
To have technology and medicine surpass us,
while not surpassing superficial insecurities.
Fear of change can be dangerous.
Everyone's history can tell you that change or
evolution is consistent.
We can't stop it; just slow it.

Pride in culture won't be lost by integration;
just evolved by embracing all cultures.
Madness you say?
Look at the children playing together;
it's done without thought.
Check history books; it was done then.
The honorable President Kennedy asked,
"What can you do for your country?"
I'm asking what you can do for yourself;
your family; and community;
other than the negative, or worse,
not doing a thing.
Let negativity die with us so the children,
will progress further,
embracing all cultures.
A universal pride learned from one another.

My Poetry

I try to write my poetry
like painters inspire for perfecting pictures.
Getting you acquainted with me;
using scenes while referring to scriptures.
My name means the "Rock."
God threw me out to hit ya.
The world is messed up!
Believe me, I'm with ya.
What you gonna do?
Stay with a closed mind?
Suffering from a sad heart?
Can't pull yourself together?
Your spirit done fell apart?
I see it as a test;
I'm about to do my best.
Gotta keep fighting; climbing;
and screaming; with my last breath.
"We are all blessed!"
Yet, in still,

"We are all cursed!"
"Only when we allow
 ourselves to be at our worst."
"Peace!"
"Only when we stop feeding the beast."

Poetry Didn't Die: It's Alive

Poetry,
as a word, has been misunderstood for no reason.
If I rhyme, I'm just reduced to a rapper.
My culture is poetic; hip hop; sonnet; literature.
Not too many read that chapter most just cool
with the banter, or many just say it
may be hard to understand,
because their cousin's friend's stepbrother
sister's roommate just read them something.
Society says it is for the stuffy and educated
people at an upscale.
Poetry has been a stable for humanity to express
the spirit; window the world; and view our souls.
Poetry has evolved in many ways;
from Prose to catchphrases
that are popular for mainstream.
Poetry never left; it is more of a reintroducing into
various styles from many artists capturing a moment.
A poet's job is to evoke emotions and illustrate
the attraction of subjects, intellectually connecting
everyone together;
being one as a cipher.

What Up

I've been to more funerals.

than weddings and graduations.

Constantly surrounded by toxic combinations

Anger; sadness of haters blissful in

bitter complacent.

Consider lazy; viewed as part of the problem.

Dining on profit for provide entertainment.

Still labeled, still viewed; and look at as crazy.

In 2004,

I wrote and published,

 "My Two Sense."

Enjoy art.

Enjoy life.

Experience love.

Angelic Reign Inc.
Est. 2004

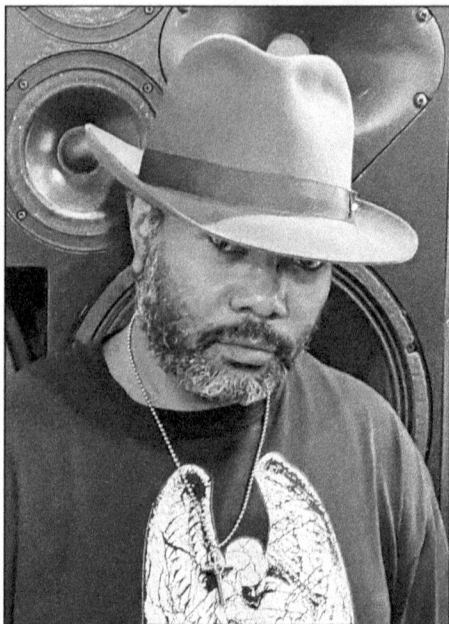

About the Author

Saint Louis, MO native Peter Cherry is an author,
songwriter; producer, publisher, and artist.
He is the co-founder of the musical group;
"KDLPC" with Kalisha D. Lemmitt-Cherry.
In 2004, Peter established, "Angelic Reign, Inc."
publishing company.
He has obtained:
Associates Degree in Communications
(St. Louis Community College-Florissant Valley);
Bachelor of Science in Media Studies
(University of Missouri Saint Louis);
Masters of Arts in Counseling
(Lindenwood University).

Out The Mud

Microphone Valley (Out The Mud)

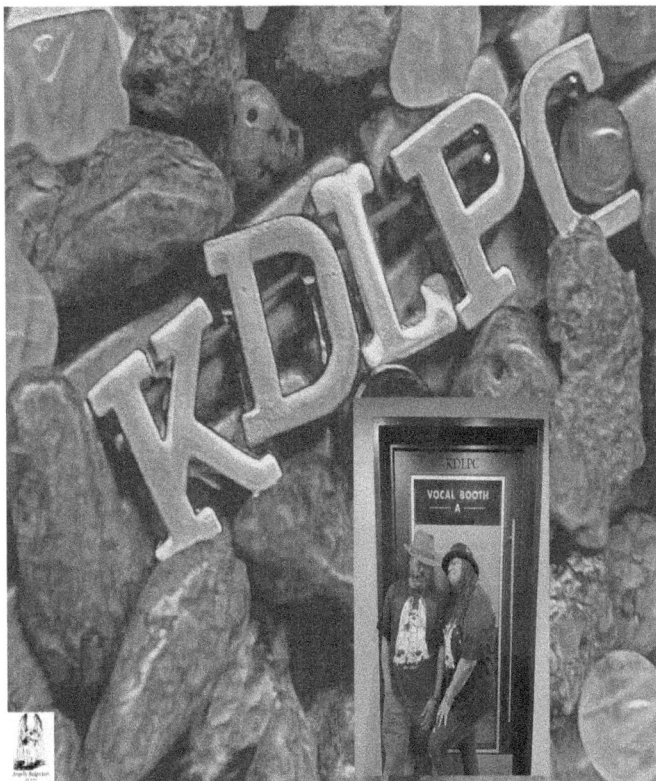

Discover new music with 'KDLPC.'